BET 7.70

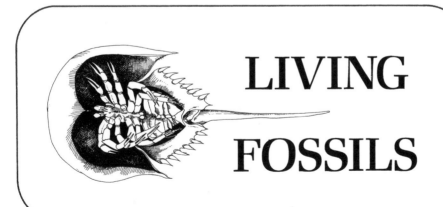

LIVING

FOSSILS

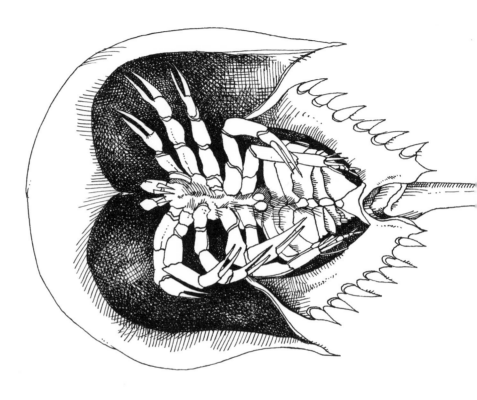

LIVING

Howard E. Smith, Jr.
Drawings by Jennifer Dewey

Dodd, Mead & Company
New York

FOSSILS

1 2 3 4 5 6 7 8 9 10

Library of Congress Cataloging in Publication Data

Smith, Howard Everett, 1927–
    Living fossils.

    Includes index.
    Summary: Describes animals either so rare or so
unusual, and with such ancient connections, that they
deserve to be known as "living fossils." Also includes
two trees which were rescued from extinction.
    1. Relicts (Biology)—Juvenile literature. 2. Animals
—Miscellanea—Juvenile literature. 3. Trees—
Miscellanea—Juvenile literature. [1. Rare animals]
I. Dewey, Jennifer, ill. II. Title.
QL49.S6534   574   82-7404
ISBN 0-396-08052-9   AACR2

For Bob

Contents

What Is a Living Fossil?

Imagine how surprising it would be if a dinosaur were discovered alive today. We could hardly imagine that a species of animal could be on earth so long—for hundreds of millions of years. We would be surprised because we know that most prehistoric animals, such as dinosaurs, pterodactyls, and other flying reptiles, together with the wooly mammoths and saber-toothed tigers, have all disappeared from the face of the earth.

But, have all the animals of the prehistoric past disappeared? And, what about the plants of those ancient times millions of years ago? All gone? Every last one of them? Oddly enough, not all of them have disappeared. Some are from times a million years before the age of the dinosaurs. Seeing them on earth today should actually be more astonishing than seeing a dinosaur. Yet we see some of these survivors from pre-historic times almost every day. Magnolia trees just like the ones that grace our lawns lived on earth at the time of the dinosaurs. In fact, dinosaurs probably ate magnolia flowers. Ginkgo trees, which now shade many city streets, were grow-ing on earth 50 million years before the first dinosaurs existed. And cockroaches ran about in forests 50 million years before the ginkgoes appeared. Although the individual insects and trees that were alive back then are not alive today, it is almost as though they were, so closely do the present-day varieties resemble their prehistoric forebears.

Such plants and animals, which look and often live just the way their ancestors did millions of years ago, are called "living fossils." Fossils are the remains or imprints of living things found in rocks, and they can form in various ways. A leaf falls into mud, leaving its imprint even after the leaf rots away. Over millions of years, the mud is compressed into stone, but it still contains the imprint. A clam dies on a sandy shore millions of years ago. As the sand is compressed into sandstone, the shell itself is embedded in the rock. A volcano erupts eons ago, covering insects or dinosaurs in hot ash, preserving their imprints or bones. All sorts of fossil remains of ancient plants and animals have been found: teeth, bones, footprints, shells, skin imprints, seeds, and pollens, among others.

A great deal of what we know about the earth's history we have learned by studying fossils—estimating their ages, examining the rock formations in which they are found, comparing them to plants and animals alive today. People who study fossils have concluded that almost all plants and animals change as time goes by. Hardly any look like their distant ancestors.

Some do, however. In fact, they look so much like the fossils we have found that it is almost as though the fossils themselves had come to life. And so we call these plants and animals "living fossils." We can learn as much or more about the past by studying them as we can by studying actual fossils.

The process by which groups of plants and animals change over time is called evolution. The description of evolution was first given by Charles Darwin, a British naturalist, in his books *The Origin of Species* (1859) and *The Descent of Man* (1871). Darwin showed that a species of animal or plant changed over time as a sort of natural selection took place among its population. He observed that there was always some variety among the members of any plant or animal group, and that certain members were more fit than others to cope with changes in their environment or in their predators or prey. These members were more likely to survive and give birth to offspring that would have similarly helpful traits. Moreover, the variations within a species often changed, too. New traits, such as longer hind legs or a crooked beak, might suddenly make their appearance as the result of a spontaneous change in the genetic makeup of an individual. Such a change is called a mutation. It can be passed on to offspring. Through the combined forces of mutation and natural selection, plants and animals evolve over time.

The first horses, for instance, were about the size of cats. Except for their heads, they did not look very much like horses. They lived in the thick underbrush of forests that grew in America about 50 million years ago. As the forests died away and were replaced by grasslands, these small mammals could no longer hide from their predators. They had to resort to running to escape from the meat-eating animals that pursued them. A natural selection in favor of the fastest runners began to take place. Slowly, over many generations, the population of horses as a whole became larger and swifter, because the ones which had traits that made them good runners were the ones which most often survived and reproduced.

A living fossil, on the other hand, is a plant or an animal which has not changed much—if at all—in millions and millions of years and has still managed to survive. For most species of plants and animals, not changing has meant extinction, the end of their life on earth forever. Some shift in climate, or change in predator, or increased competition has wiped them out before helpful adaptations could evolve. But living fossils have survived *despite* the fact that they have not changed throughout the ages. This is not because all living fossils are swift and powerful. Many of them are not. Actually, no one can say for sure why some species of living things last so long without changing. But if an animal or plant gets enough to eat, lives in a place that does not change very much, and is not killed off by predators or a calamity, it may have a chance at becoming a living fossil. A small insect like the silverfish is a living fossil that has remained unchanged on earth for 250 million years. It survives not because it is strong, powerful, or smart, but because it always seems to find enough to eat, is not bothered too much by enemies, and lives in warm forests that have had more or less the same climate for millions of years. Most of the dragonflies we see today have not changed much, except for size, in 320 million years, so well are they adapted to their lifestyles and environments.

Of the living fossils on earth, the ones which follow are an interesting sampling.

The World's Oldest Tree

———— • ◄◄◄ • ————

THE GINKGO

One of the most awesome sights on earth is a glacier moving through a forest. Millions of tons of ice slowly break trees down and scour the land clean of any living thing.

During the Ice Ages, which lasted from about fifty thousand years ago to eleven thousand years ago, huge glaciers periodically spread across the northern parts of Europe and America. These glaciers were probably the largest in the history of the planet, at times extending from present-day Alaska all the way to what is now Kentucky. In many places, the ice was over a mile deep.

On the continents of Europe and North America, the glaciers killed pines, birches, maples, and many other types of trees. But as the climate gradually grew warmer, the glaciers retreated and these trees grew back. They were able to do so because the same kinds of trees farther south had escaped the glaciers, and winds or animals had carried their seeds northward.

The glaciers also killed off another kind of tree in Europe and America, the ginkgo tree. But after the glaciers retreated, no ginkgoes grew back, because none had ever grown south of where the glaciers stopped. After the glaciers, there were no ginkgoes anywhere in Europe or America.

There were ginkgo trees in China, however. The glaciers of the Ice Ages covered only high mountains in China, and the rest of the land remained free of them. The ginkgo trees there continued to grow in the wild. No one knows how many there were; probably it was never a common tree.

At some time in China's long history, people began to plant ginkgoes in order to harvest their fruit, which is edible when cooked, although when raw it may be poisonous. (Never eat one!) As centuries went by, more and more ginkgoes were grown in orchards; eventually very few grew in the wild. Then, about a thousand years ago, the Chinese stopped growing ginkgoes for their fruit and instead began raising trees such as the apple and pear, which have bigger and better fruit. All the ginkgoes in the world might have died off, except that the Chinese had a feeling of reverence for the trees. Buddhist priests grew them in and around temple courtyards.

In the sixth century A.D., upperclass Japanese became enchanted with the Chinese T'ang dynasty and brought to their country Chinese artists, writers, philosophers, and Chinese Buddhist priests. These priests took some ginkgo trees with them and planted sacred groves near the temples they established. Today some of the finest and biggest ginkgoes grow in Japan. A few are over one hundred feet high and have trunks twenty-four feet in diameter, about the size of a very large oak.

Up until the fifteenth century, no European had ever seen a ginkgo tree. Then travelers to the Orient in the fifteenth and sixteenth centuries began to mention them in their writings. In 1690 Engelbert Kaempfer, a German, went to Japan. He drew pictures of ginkgoes, which appeared in his book, *History of Japan and Siam*, published in 1728. Around 1730, an unknown Dutchman brought a small ginkgo tree back to Utrecht, Holland, and planted it. It grew very well. Today, an old ginkgo in Utrecht may be that very same one.

In 1784, a Frenchman, Andre Michaux, brought some ginkgo tree to America. They were planted in Philadelphia. Several wealthy people, Thomas Jefferson among them, took an interest in the trees. Gradually, estates, botanic gardens, and a few city parks grew them, mainly as curiosities. Once the trees were large, it was evident that they were not as bothered by insects as most other trees, and that no fungi grew on them. City planners, searching for tough, hardy trees which could withstand insect and fungus attacks, began planting ginkgoes in most American cities. Today they decorate many city streets and parks. It has also been discovered that ginkgo trees are not as affected by pollution as are other trees, and so they have been planted in urban areas all over the world. They are becoming one of the most common trees of all.

During the eighteenth century, the science of botany advanced rapidly, and botanists studying trees and other plants realized that the ginkgo tree was unique in many respects. Unlike other trees, male ginkgo trees produce motile sperm, which land on the pulpy watery fruit of female trees and fertilize them. The tree is also different from other trees in the way its trunk and limbs grow. Compared to other trees, it has only a few large limbs. Most botanists feel that ginkgoes are in some way related to pines. The fan-shaped leaves look very much like a bundle of pine needles with green webbing between them.

When Charles Darwin proposed the theory of evolution, he described the ginkgo tree as a "living fossil" and thereby coined the phrase. Indeed, the ginkgo is the world's oldest "woody" tree, which means that its wood is made up of annual rings. Most American trees have such rings. Trees with softer wood and no annual rings, such as palms, cycads, and bamboos, are called herbaceous trees.

Fossils of ginkgo trees go back millions of years. Ernest H.

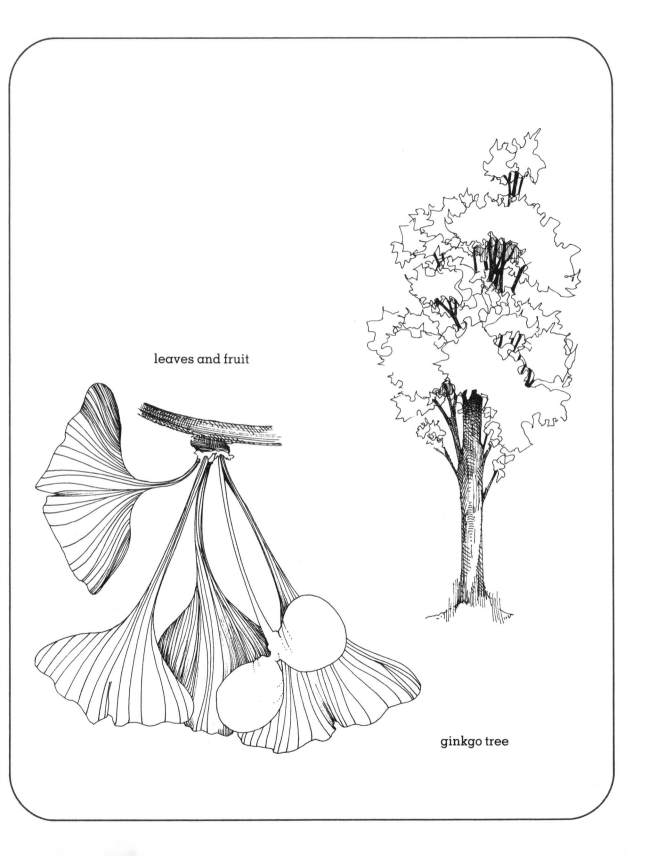

leaves and fruit

ginkgo tree

Wilson, keeper of the Arnold Arboretum of Harvard University, speculates that the trees themselves may possibly date from the Carboniferous period, which began 345 million years ago. The ginkgo shares a particular characteristic with plants from the Carboniferous period. Many plants back then reproduced by way of motile sperm, the way the ginkgo does. Since no large tree of any sort appears to have used motile sperm as a means of reproduction after the Carboniferous period, it is unlikely that the ginkgo appeared on earth later than that time. Yet we have no direct fossil evidence for its appearance during that period.

The Strangest Mammal

THE DUCKBILL PLATYPUS

In 1799, Dr. George Shaw, a curator at the British Museum in London, received a package from Australia. When he opened it, he found the skin of a very unusual animal. At first glance, it looked like the skin of a mammal, for it was covered with fur, and only mammals have fur. But the head of the animal had a bill that looked like a duck's bill. That was puzzling. How could a mammal have a bill like a bird?

Shaw could not believe it. For a while he and other scientists thought the skin might be a hoax. People had played tricks with animals before. They had sewn monkey heads on fish and sold them as mermaids. Had someone sewn a duck's bill onto the skin of an unknown animal?

British scientists examined the skin very carefully and found that nothing was sewn together. It was obviously the skin of a genuine animal, completely new to science. But what sort of animal was it? There was disagreement about that. Some scientists pointed out that if the animal were a mammal, the mother would produce milk. But how could a young mammal suck milk with a bill? A few scientists thought it might be a reptile. Some prehistoric reptiles, such as the duck-billed dinosaurs, had had bills.

To make matters worse, the British Museum received another duckbilled "mammal." It was a female, but she did not have any teats for the young to suckle. She did not have any mammary glands either. The mystery deepened.

In 1824, a German professor, J. F. Meckelt, was in Australia and saw a live duckbilled mammal for himself and discovered that it laid eggs. He also discovered that although the animal did not have either teats or mammary glands, the female did produce milk. It oozed out of the skin at her belly and the young lapped it up. Meckelt's findings complicated matters more than ever.

The animal, by then called a duckbill platypus, became the focus of heated debates among scientists. For years they argued about it. Those who chose to call it a reptile pointed out that it laid eggs, had a bill, and had no teeth. Reptiles laid eggs and a few rare reptiles were known to have bills. Moreover, all birds, which are close relatives of reptiles, have bills

duckbill platypus

and no teeth, but most mammals have teeth. Many scientists, seeing that the argument could go on forever, suggested placing the animal in a class all by itself. Today, the duckbill platypus is called a mammal, but few are satisfied with that classification.

After Charles Darwin proposed his theory of evolution, the duckbill platypus became a more significant animal in the eyes of many scientists. The theory of evolution claims that mammals must have evolved from reptiles. Evidence from fossils indicates that this is so, and the duckbill platypus gives us a good living example. It is an excellent link between reptiles and mammals.

The reproduction cycle of the duckbill interests scientists the most, for it is unlike that of other mammals. All others give birth to live young. But the female duckbill lays eggs, as do reptiles. She lays them deep inside a burrow where they will be safe. When the eggs hatch, the female lies on her back and the young crawl on her. Their motion causes milk to ooze from her body and the young lap it up.

Today, duckbills are found in streams in southern Australia and in Tasmania. For their two-foot size, these animals make extremely long burrows, some reaching fifty feet in length, in the banks of rivers and streams. The duckbill builds its burrow so narrow that it can hardly squeeze through. There is an interesting reason for this. The sides of the burrow act as a towel.

When a duckbill wiggles through after swimming in the water, its fur is squeezed dry.

The duckbill eats small fish, worms, and freshwater clams. It is voracious, consuming more than its weight in food each day. Those in zoos must be fed almost all the time. In the wild the duckbill is an excellent hunter. Although it has good sight and hearing, it usually hunts underwater in murky places. There its bill proves useful. The bill is not hard, as many people think. It becomes hard if the animal is dead, but when the animal is alive, the bill is soft and filled with very sensitive nerves. Using its bill, the duckbill feels for things in the murky streams where it feeds.

Duckbills look like cuddly little animals that would make cute pets. Actually, they are very dangerous. The males have spurs on their hind legs which are connected to poison glands. A stab from a spur can make a man's arm swell up and leave him feeling sick for months.

Duckbill fossils date from almost two million years ago. Because it seems to be such a primitive mammal, closely related to reptiles, scientists feel sure that much older fossils must exist. The duckbill may even go back to the age of the dinosaurs, which ended sixty million years ago.

No one knows exactly why the duckbill has survived for such a long time, but it has several things in its favor. First of all, it lived in Australia and Tasmania. These two places have been separated from Asia, and from all other large land masses, for at least 100 million years. Animals in Australia and Tasmania were protected from predators such as leopards, wolves, and foxes. No such powerful, quick, and intelligent animals ever hunted the duckbills. Secondly, because the duckbill is such a good swimmer, it could easily escape any predators that might be around. It could also retreat into its burrow, and the poison spurs would discourage any enemies. All of these factors have probably helped it survive.

The Oldest Living Animal Fossil

NEOPILINA GALATHEA

What is the oldest living animal fossil on earth? It is a small mollusk called *Neopilina galathea*. It has lived on earth for about 550 million years.

Mollusks are animals that have soft bodies which are protected, in almost all cases, by a hard shell. Typical mollusks are clams, oysters, snails, and abalones. A few, like squid, octopuses, and slugs, lack shells. *Neopilina* has a one-inch-long shell, round and shaped like a conical cap, on top of its body. Yellowish-white on the outside and shiny mother-of-pearl on the inside, the shell is so thin that light can go through it.

The discovery of this ancient living fossil came as a complete surprise. On May 6, 1952, a Danish research ship, the

Galathea, was sailing off the Pacific coast of Central America on a round-the-world cruise. Scientists on board hoisted a catch from the ocean bottom 11,778 feet below. Among the animals they brought up were ten small mollusks, which were initially identified as snails. As it was a hot, tiring day, no one paid further attention to the mollusks. They were preserved in jars, however, which would be brought back to Denmark for examination later.

It can take months, years, or even decades for the material collected on one scientific expedition to be catalogued, studied, and fully understood. In this sense, the *Galathea* was like most others. Years afterward, biologists were still busy working on the collection of plants and animals the journey had produced, to find out *exactly* what they had.

In August, 1956, Dr. Henning Lemche of the *Galathea* expedition began examining the "snails." As he looked at the small mollusks, he realized that they were actually not snails. Outwardly they did resemble certain types of snails, but their inner structure was not snail-like. In fact, the mollusks were in some ways so different from any other animal Lemche was familiar with that he asked other researchers to help him determine what they were. Together they looked at drawings and photographs of possible relatives.

After a careful investigation, they concluded that the mollusks were not closely related to any living animal. Were they

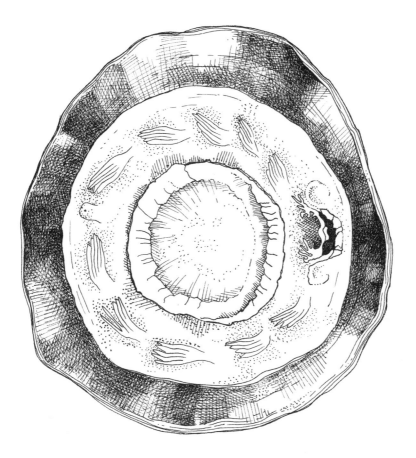

Neopilina galathea

perhaps related to an extinct animal? A fossil might show that. Numerous fossils and drawings of fossils were examined. The scientists finally came across a group of fossil mollusks in the class Monoplacophora. One was named *Pilina*. They obtained the fossil and carefully examined the shell, which was all they had, since the animal's soft body had rotted away millions of years ago. The shell told them a great deal about the *Pilina*, however. They could see places where *Pilina's* muscles had been attached. In all details the shell matched the shells of the mollusks brought aboard the *Galathea*. Instead of finding a fossil relative, they appeared to have found the animal itself! To their amazement, they had discovered the world's oldest living animal fossil.

The scientists gave the living animal a name, *Neopilina galathea*. "Neo" means new, the word *galathea*, of course, came from the name of the research ship.

Scientists on other ships in the Pacific and Indian oceans searched for more *Neopilinas* and found them. They all lived in deep waters, mostly over two miles down. The vast majority of marine animals live in water which is less than five hundred feet deep. Most plant life, an indispensable part of the marine ecosystem, can grow to about that depth because sunlight reaches that far underwater. In some places it reaches about a thousand feet down, but at that depth the light is too dim to support much plant life.

Not many animals live in deeper waters, because there is simply far less food there. Most animals that live deep depend on the remains of microscopic plants and animals that grow on the surface of the waves, and the remains of a few fish and other large animals. These fall to the bottom of the sea where the animals scavenge them. No one knows exactly what the *Neopilina* eats, except that it eats what falls to the bottom of the sea.

Of course, the most interesting thing about the *Neopilina galathea* is that it has lived on earth so long. Its fossil relatives go back 550 million years to the Cambrian period.

A Household Master at Survival

———— ·◄►· ————

THE COCKROACH

The cockroach has at least one claim to fame. Of all the animals, it was the first to fly.

When the winged ancestors of today's cockroaches first appeared, the world was covered with many huge swamps. The air was damp and hot and smelled of rotting vegetation. Giant ferns and club mosses, cycads and horsetail rushes, made up the earth's forests. Primitive reptiles crawled on the ground, and huge scorpions scuttled about. This period 300 million years ago is known as the Carboniferous period. Cockroaches have not changed much since then.

Cockroaches are often called "masters at survival." (If you have ever tried to squash one, you will know why.) But in fact, all living fossils are masters at survival; generations of them

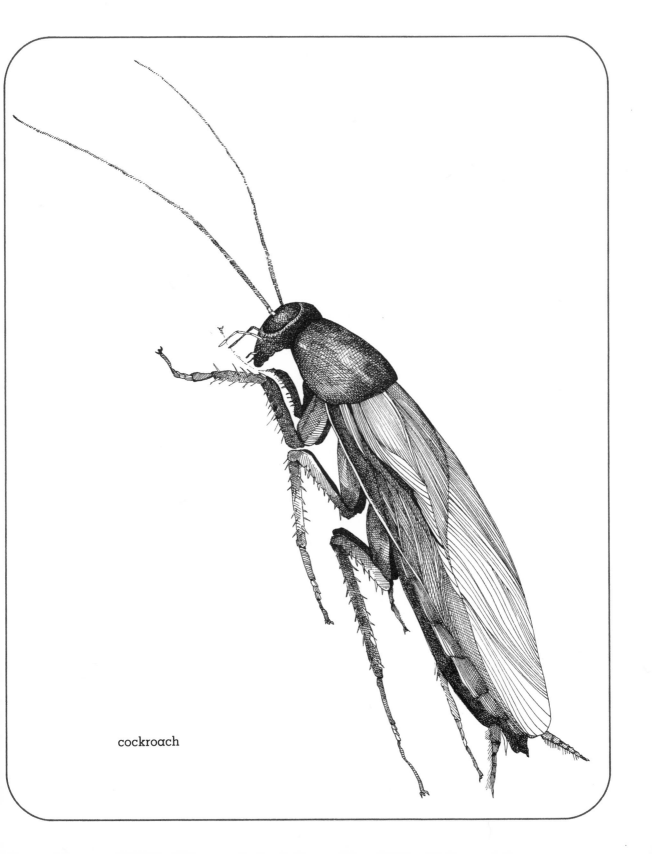

cockroach

have continued to live, grow, and reproduce for millions of years. Otherwise these animals and plants would not be *living* fossils today.

When biologists speak of the success of an animal, however, they are usually concerned with its population and distribution. In both these respects, cockroaches are enormously successful. There are billions of them on earth, from Canada to Cape Horn, from France to Australia. Under natural conditions, cockroaches live primarily in tropical forests, but human beings have carried some species all over the world (usually aboard ship) and unwittingly provided them with warm habitats in which they are able to survive otherwise forbidding environments. The nooks and crannies of heated buildings protect them only too well from the freezing temperatures of a New York City winter, for instance.

Very few animals inhabit so many places, especially in such great numbers. This widespread and populous distribution guarantees the cockroach a long future, since it would be difficult to wipe them out in every area at once. It appears that they are here to stay.

What traits make cockroaches so successful? First of all, they can, and will, eat almost anything: rotting wood, fungi, eggs, meat, vegetables, you name it. If one source of food disappears, a cockroach can always find another. Furthermore, in comparison with other insects, cockroaches are swift runners, and they have extremely sensitive hairs on their tail ends, which serve as a warning system that propels their swift legs into action.

The sensory hairs are actually wind receptors (440 in all), and they respond to puffs of air of the sort that are created when a toad lunges at a cockroach or when someone begins a fast swipe through the air to hit one. Each sensory hair is connected to a nerve, and when a puff of air bends a few hairs, nerve impulses are generated which somehow turn the cockroach away from the source of the puff and start it moving. Under the best conditions, a cockroach can be off and running within eleven milliseconds of the time its hairs are activated.

That's very fast. Perhaps these insects indeed deserve the title "masters at survival."

Beach Invaders from Another Time

THE HORSESHOE CRAB

On summer nights when the moon is full, tens of thousands of male horseshoe crabs come ashore along the beaches of the eastern United States. They wait and, later in the night, female horseshoe crabs come to the beaches. The males mount the females and fertilize the eggs the females lay. It looks like an invasion from the ocean's depths. Actually, it is an invasion from the past. For at least 250 million years horseshoe crabs have been coming to shore like this to mate.

Despite their name and their physical resemblance to crabs, these animals are not crabs. They are arachnids, a group of animals that includes spiders, ticks, and scorpions. The horseshoe crab's closest relatives are ticks and scorpions, but they are also related to two fascinating extinct animals. One is the

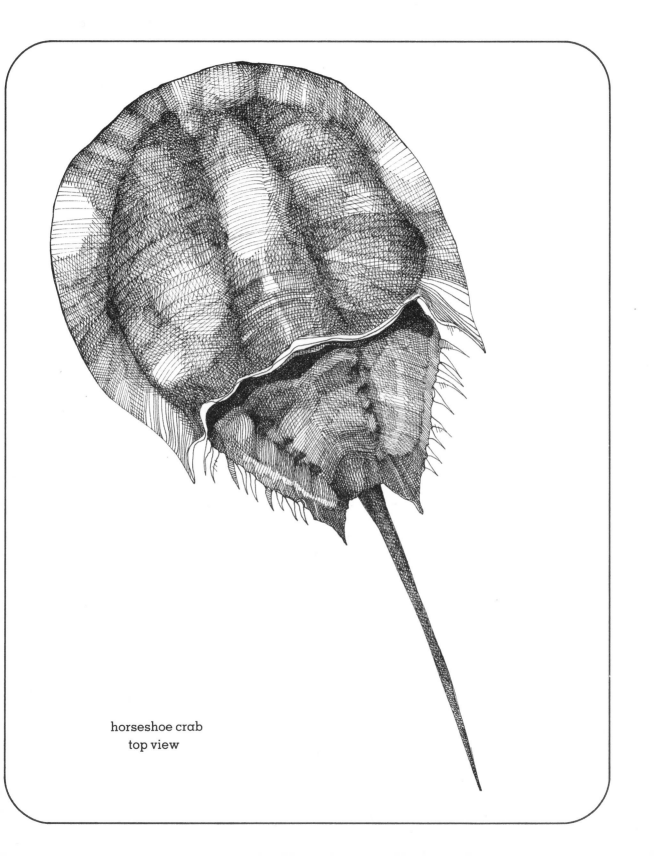

horseshoe crab
top view

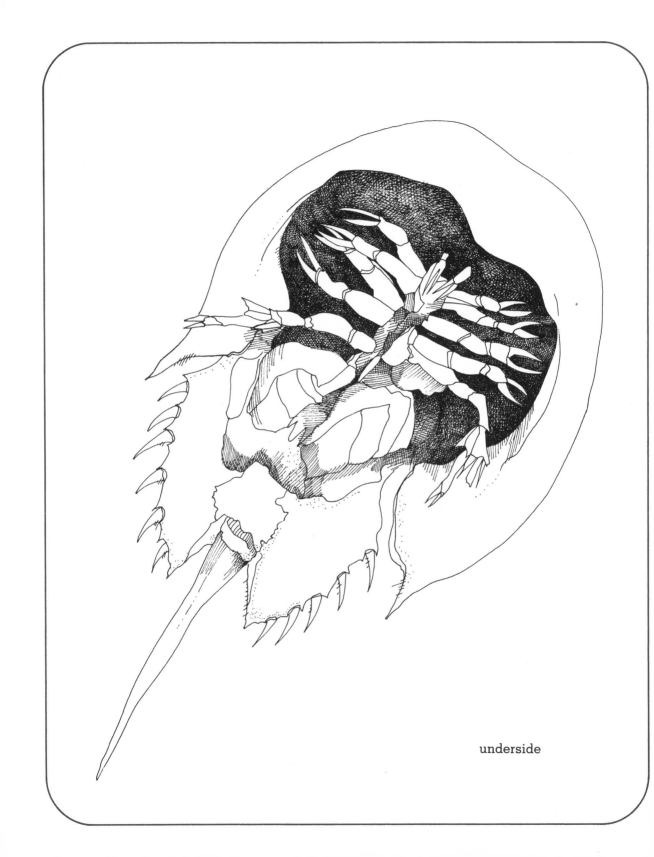

underside

trilobite, which appeared on earth during the Cambrian period about 550 million years ago and became extinct about 300 million years ago. Trilobites were once among the largest, strongest, and most common animals on earth. The other is the eurypterid, which also appeared on earth during the Cambrian period. Eurypterids looked a bit like scorpions, although much larger.

We cannot see living trilobites any more, but we can see something that looks almost exactly like them—the young, or larvae, of horseshoe crabs. When the larvae change and grow and become adult horseshoe crabs, they bear only a vague resemblance to trilobites. The horseshoe crabs do not seem to be direct descendants of the trilobites, although obviously they are closely related.

Today horsehoe crabs are extremely common. Over a million have been known to gather in one mile of beach. They come ashore in the summer, and during the rest of the year they stay in the ocean, never far from shore. Oddly enough, they swim upside down, with their legs pointed up toward the surface of the water. If they happen to land on shore that way, they must turn themselves over and get their legs under them so they can walk. They flip over by pushing against the sand with their long, pointed tails.

The horseshoe crab has been useful in certain zoological studies. Dr. A. J. Carlson studied the hearts of horseshoe crabs.

Before his work, scientists had wondered whether a heart beats because its muscles contract by themselves, or whether a nerve impluse from the brain or from someplace else in the body is necessary to trigger the heart muscles. It was difficult to ascertain the answer, for the hearts of highly developed animals and humans are affected by nerve impulses from many different places in their bodies. Horseshoe crabs were studied because they have a very small brain and very few nerves. Their hearts are free of interfering impulses. As it turned out, the horseshoe crab's heart muscles beat on their own and did not need nerve impulses to stimulate them.

Living fossils allow scientists to see how "primitive" animals and plants, those that are very old in terms of the earth's history, may have looked. Because they came first, primitive plants and animals are generally simpler in structure than more evolved animals. Often scientists want to look at simpler structures in order to better understand more complicated ones. The horseshoe crab has been useful in just such a dual fashion.

The "Man" Who Saw the Flood

THE GIANT SALAMANDER

We know about living fossils because we know about fossils. But there was a time, two hundred years ago and earlier, when people did not even know what fossils were.

In the seventeenth and eighteenth centuries, naturalists argued over what had caused the shapes and imprints in rocks that looked like living things. Were they just natural impressions that happened to look like bones or shells? Some people thought so. But the majority considered them to be antediluvain remains. The word "antediluvian" is not heard too much these days, but it means "before the flood." The naturalists believed that fossils were the remains of plants and animals that lived before the Biblical flood, the one that Noah's ark survived. As they saw it, the flood had swept across the world, covering plants and animals with mud, which eventually turned to rock and formed the fossils.

One man who believed this was J. J. Scheuzer. One day in 1726 he came across a fascinating fossil in the hills near Basel, Switzerland. It looked like a human skeleton, and he was sure that it was the fossil of a man. He collected it and called it *Homo antediluvii testis*, which means "the man who witnessed the flood." The fossil was greatly admired by other naturalists, who felt that an ancient man had been discoverd. They figured the man had drowned in B.C. 2603, the year the Church believed the flood had taken place.

In spite of its looks, the fossil was not at all human. It was actually the fossil of a giant salamander, an animal that had witnessed a world far more ancient than any human could have witnessed. It had roamed the earth about 250 million years ago. The giant salamander was older than the crocodiles, the dinosaurs, or any reptile, for that matter.

The recognition of *Homo antediluvii testis's* true identity began in 1820. Phillipe Franz Van Siebold, a German physician and naturalist, was in Japan searching for unusual plants and animals. One day while walking in a market, he came across what was to him a perplexing sight. Butchers were selling animals that looked like salamanders, only they were gigantic. When Siebold realized that the animals actually were salamanders, he was shocked. All the salamanders he had ever

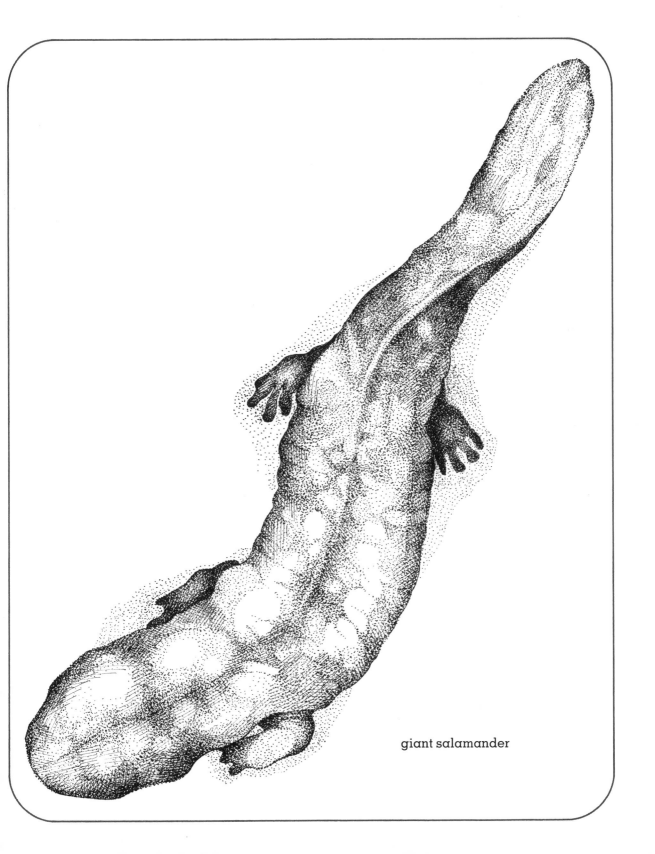

giant salamander

seen or heard about were only a few inches long. But those in the Japanese market were over four feet long. Siebold realized that these animals were unknown to European naturalists. He asked the Japanese where the salamanders came from, and they explained that the animals lived in mountain streams. Siebold set off to find them.

In 1829 Siebold took a male and female giant salamander back to Europe. Examining them, naturalists were reminded of the fossil *Homo antediluvii testis*. A quick check of the fossil skeleton revealed the truth. It was not human after all, but the fossil of a giant salamander.

The naturalists who had been so awed by the fossil called *Homo antediluvii testis*, believing it to be four thousand years old, would have been amazed at its true age. It was 250 million years old.

The male and female salamanders were put in a zoo. Unfortunately, they were fed inappropriate food and eventually the hungry male ate the female. The zoo keepers finally hit upon the right food, and the male lived for fifty-five years in captivity. We do not know how old the salamander was when it arrived at the zoo, but obviously its life-span was longer than fifty-five years. This suggests that giant salamanders are long-lived animals; some may even be a hundred years old.

On land, the giant salamander is the oldest living fossil with a backbone. No other land-dwelling vertebrate goes so far back in the earth's history. Today there are still giant salamanders in Japan, living under weeds in surprisingly small streams, into which they barely fit. Unfortunately, like so many animals, the giant salamanders are endangered by modern civilization, as towns and factories encroach upon their habitats. It is too bad that after inhabiting our planet for so long, the oldest land vertebrate of all may someday become extinct.

The Long Hunt

THE OKAPI

About 160 years ago, the Frenchman Georges Cuvier, considered one of the world's greatest zoologists, declared that no more large animals unknown to science would ever be discovered. He was mistaken, because several large animals have been found since then. One of the most interesting of all is the okapi.

In the late nineteenth century, European and American explorers were probing the interior of Africa, which had up until then been largely unknown to the outside world. The most famous explorer of all was probably Sir Henry Stanley. In 1871 he went deep into Africa to find the missing missionary, David Livingston. Stanley wrote a book about his adventures, *In Darkest Africa*, which became a best-seller. In it he mentioned that Pygmies had told him they sometimes captured wild don-keys in deep pits.

When the zoologist Sir Harry Johnston read Stanley's book, he wondered what animals the Pygmies had actually cap-tured. He felt sure it could not have been donkeys. The Pygmies lived in the Congo Forest in today's Zaire, one of the largest and gloomiest jungles in the world. Johnston thought that no horses, zebras, or donkeys could live there because of its dense tropical vegetation. Those animals live on open plains. It would have been as unlikely to find a donkey in the Congo Forest as it would be to find a polar bear in Arizona.

Johnston suspected that the Pygmies had captured a large animal thus far unknown to science. For them to have called it a donkey probably meant that it looked like the donkeys they had seen with explorers or traders. It all added up to one thing: there was a great discovery to be made in Africa.

Johnston lost no time getting to the Congo Forest. In 1900 he questioned Pygmies about the strange animal. The pygmies called the animal an *okhapi*. Other Africans, the Bambuba, called it an *okapi*. Some pygmies said they could get the skin of one, but when they went to get it, they found that it had been cut up into belts. Only a small piece was left. Johnston sent it to London

At the December, 1900, meeting of the Zoological Society in London, some of the best zoologists in the world passed the skin around to each other for careful examination. Judging from the type of leather and hair, they decided that it came from an animal related to a horse, and they gave it the scientific name *Equus johnstoni*. In Latin, *equus* means horse.

The hunt for the okapi intensified. One was shot. This time the complete skin and skull were sent to London, and the zoologists realized that the okapi was closely related to a giraffe, although it did not have such long legs or such a long neck, and was about the size of a moose. The name *Equus Johnstoni* was quietly discarded for a new name, *Okapia johnstoni*, and that is what we call it today.

News of the animal spread around the world. Zoologists were stunned, and newspapers gave headlines to the newly discovered animal. People everywhere were excited. Plans were made to catch one alive for a zoo.

As scientists studied the skin and skull, however, they began to wonder whether fossil bones of okapis hadn't already been found. Was the okapi really so new to science? Perhaps the animal itself was an exciting discovery, but weren't there already fossils of it? Could it be a living fossil?

In 1853, George Finlay, an Englishman, had done what quite a few wealthy Englishmen of the time were doing. He had gone to Greece to "dig," to look for lost Grecian statues, art objects, and other remains of the great ancient Greek civilizations.

Finlay had gone to Pikermi and had had no luck finding

okapi mother and young

Greek remains, but he did discover a number of odd-looking bones of prehistoric animals. He realized that they might interest paleontologists, so he invited some to come join him. The scientists observed that the bones seemed to be mainly from animals of the type found in Africa today. During the Pliocene period, which began 12 million years ago when the climate was warmer, many animals roamed across Europe. At a much later date the climate grew colder, and the animals either died or migrated into what is now Africa. That was easy to do, for the Mediterranean Sea was dry land then.

The paleontologists in Pikermi had found many bones which they thought belonged to extinct animals. One such animal they had named Helladotherium, which means "Hellas animal"; Hellas is another name for Greece. The Helladotherium was obviously related to a giraffe, but it had a shorter neck and shorter legs.

Later, at the turn of the century, zoologists compared the skull of the okapi with a fossil skull of Helladotherium. There was no doubt about it. They were one and the same species. The okapi of the Congo Forest was a 12 million-year-old living fossil—almost. In 1901, no one outside of Africa had seen a living okapi. So, to be more exact, the okapi was a living fossil yet to be seen alive by Europeans.

But how would one set about seeing a living okapi? The Congo Forest was not a place to go hunting—not in the early

1900s. It extended 1,800 miles across Africa, and most of it was unexplored. Moreover, it was one of the most miserable jungles in the world. Night and day the temperature stayed near a steamy 100° F. Insects threatened explorers with diseases, most of which, in those days, had no known cure.

No one knew how many okapis were in the Congo Forest. In most of the dense jungle, a person could hardly see ten feet in any direction, so the okapi could easily hide. A large land animal could not have chosen a better place to escape hunters. Indeed, the okapi proved to be extremely elusive.

A few okapis were eventually shot by natives and their skins sent to museums. Then, in 1909, Hubert Lang of the Bronx Zoo saw an okapi and captured it, only to have it die a few days later. Soon explorers learned that okapis rarely stayed alive more than a few days after they were caught. Approximately thirty-five years went by and still no one was able to bring a living okapi out of Africa.

Sixty-six years after Stanley had heard of the okapi, one was finally captured which did not die right away. On November 4, 1935, natives trapped a very young okapi. It was raised in Africa for a few years and then sent to the Bronx Zoo. It arrived on August 18, 1937, and became a smash hit with the public. One of the longest and most difficult hunts in history had ended. For a long time Lang was given credit for being the first non-African to see a living okapi. But was he? Sir Harry Johnston, who had obtained the first skin, was not so sure. He carefully reread the notes Stanley had taken while he was in Africa. In them, Stanley mentioned watching a large unknown mammal near the Semiliki River. Johnston discussed the animal with Stanley, raising the possibility that it had been an opaki, but Stanley could not give a positive answer. From the evidence, however, Johnston concluded that Stanley rather than Lang was the first explorer to have seen a live okapi.

The Animal with Three Eyes

THE TUATARA

The tuatara is surely one of the most unusual animals on earth. It is a reptile with three eyes. Its third eye is on top of its head.

During the Permian period, which began 280 million years ago, a group of reptiles that had three eyes developed. One such reptile was the moschops, which lived in the area that is today South Africa. Most three-eyed reptiles became extinct, but the tuatara survived. It has been on earth for 225 million years. On the Galápagos Islands there is a black lizard that also has three eyes, but its third eye does not have sight. Although the tuatara's third eye is quite weak, it can distinguish light and dark.

The story of the tuatara is a good example of how some animals are able to survive for very long periods of time because they happen to live on remote islands where they are safe from enemies. The tuatara now lives on islands off the shore of New Zealand, hundreds of miles from land, but at one time tuataras were quite common in the region that is today called Asia. Eventually, however, the ones there were wiped out by predators. If some tuataras had not also been living on land that is now part of New Zealand, none would be alive today.

How did the tuatara get to New Zealand? During the Jurassic period, which began 181 million years ago, the oceans were much lower than they are now, and the land that is now called New Zealand was not a group of islands. It was connected to Asia by a strip of land, and the tuatara walked to New Zealand. When the seas rose a few million years later, New Zealand became a group of islands. The tuataras were thereby protected from all the fierce predators which would subsequently evolve in Asia. No Asian dinosaurs, tigers, or foxes would ever bother them—after all, how would they get there?

Unfortunately, the tuataras were not to be protected forever. When white settlers first arrived in New Zealand, tuataras lived everywhere on New Zealand's two large islands and its many smaller, offshore islands. The settlers brought pigs with them. Although no one thinks of pigs as fierce predators, the pigs hunted the tuataras and ate them. They killed off all the tuataras that lived on the two big islands. Today, tuataras live only on some small offshore islands.

tuatara

People who have seen tuataras report that they are about the slowest animals imaginable. They may not move for hours at a time. They breathe so slowly that it can take one over an hour to draw a single breath. They spend most of their time in holes or sunning themselves on rocks. The Maoris, who were the original inhabitants of New Zealand, say that some tuataras lived for three hundred years. If so, they have the longest life spans of animals living on earth. It is known that they can live well over a hundred years.

Tuataras are an endangered species. The New Zealand government has tried to protect its remaining tuataras, but thieves sneak out to the uninhabited islands, catch them, and ship them to distant ports. Today some are sold for $10,000 apiece in New York City.

This is a shameful business. The tuatara, the oldest living fossil reptile, takes us back to a remote period of time. Moreover, no other animal on earth is anything like it. It would be terrible to see the tuatara become extinct after having survived 225 million years because a few selfish, unthinking people desire an exotic pet.

America's Only Marsupial

THE OPOSSUM

The opossum is one of North America's most interesting animals because it is America's only marsupial. Marsupials are mammals whose females carry their young in pouches. There are many marsupials in the world, but almost all of them live in Australia and Tasmania. Some of the common Australian marsupials are koala bears, wombats, and kangaroos.

It is thought that the earliest mammals were egg layers, like the duckbill platypus. These early egg-laying mammals evolved from reptiles. From the egg layers, two new and different groups of mammals evolved, both at about the same time. These are the two mammal groups we are familiar with today.

One group, the marsupials, gives birth to extremely tiny, undeveloped young. A kangaroo, for instance, is hardly more than an inch long and completely helpless at birth, yet it must crawl along its mother's belly to her pouch. Once inside the pouch, it tightens its lips around one of her nipples, and contractions of the muscles above the nipple squirt milk into its mouth. A newborn marsupial remains in its mother's pouch until it can fend for itself—often a matter of months.

The other group of mammals is the placentals. Placental young are born at a far more advanced stage of development than marsupial young. A placental baby grows inside its mother's body, where its needs are met by a special organ called a placenta, which delivers nutrients and oxygen from the mother's body and carries away waste materials. The baby is not born until it is quite well developed. A newborn placental mammal, a calf, for instance, is far more able to take care of itself than an inch-long kangaroo.

Placental mammals were a great success. In almost all places on earth where there were both marsupial and placental mammals, the placentals displaced the marsupials. In Australia, however, marsupials thrived, because placentals somehow never reached this large island continent. Two kinds of marsupials in South America also managed to survive. One is the rare caenolestes of the Andes Mountains. The other is the family Didelphidae, of which the common opossum is the most familiar member.

At one time North and South America were separated by

opossum

ocean; the land bridge at Panama did not exist. While the two continents were separated, very different sorts of animals developed in both places. In general the animals of North America were tougher and smarter, especially the carnivores (meat eaters). When the land bridge formed, wolves, coyotes, pumas, and other placental mammals poured into South America. They wiped out one marsupial species after another.

In spite of this, the common opossum not only survived the onslaught, it actually pushed into North America, proving to be one of the very few South American animals to do so.

When Columbus and other explorers arrived in the New World, Europeans had never seen marsupials; they did not even know such animals existed. In 1500, the explorer Vincente Yanez Pinzon, who had commanded the *Niña* on Columbus's expedition, brought a female opossum back to Spain from Brazil and presented it to Queen Isabella I and King Ferdinand V. They were absolutely fascinated with the animal and stuck their bejeweled fingers into its pouch. Several writers of the time—Peter Martyr, Angelo Trevigliano, and Richard Eden— told the story of this new animal curiosity. Many people wanted to read about it and see drawings of it, so the opossum's "fame" spread.

The opossum is said to have gotten its rather unusual name from Captain John Smith's interpretation of an Indian word. Captain Smith was a leader of the Jamestown settlement, and in 1612 he saw some opossums in Virginia. He asked the local Indians what they called the animals, and they spoke a name which meant "white face." Our word opossum is close in sound to the Indian word.

Today the population of the common opossum is increasing, a rather surprising development when you consider the odds against the opossum having survived at all. To begin with, it has a very tiny brain for a mammal of its size. A cat, a placental mammal of comparable size, has a brain that is four times as large. Moreover, the cat's brain is more highly developed, so there is reason to believe that the cat is considerably more intelligent.

Then why does the opossum gain in number? There is no exact explanation, but there would seem to be several reasons for it. In comparison with other mammals, the opossum has a high birth rate. A female can give birth to as many as twenty-two opossums at one time (although she only has eleven to thirteen nipples, so some newborn members of such a large litter will not live). Opossums spend their days well protected inside hollow trees, and they look for food at night, where darkness, as well as their habit of "playing dead," gives them protection from enemies. And opossums can, and do, eat almost anything: fruits, vegetables, mice, and insects. Since Americans leave a good deal of litter and garbage around, an opossum hunting at night can almost always find a good meal.

Furthermore, the opossum's natural enemies, such as foxes, bobcats, and large snakes, are decreasing. This is because people have hunted them and because people have taken over their habitats, building stores, homes, and parking lots where these animals once lived. One of the surest ways to kill off a species is to deny it a place to live.

The opossum and the gingko tree are two living fossils making a great comeback in America. There was once a theory that the genes of living fossils become tired and worn out. Happily, that theory itself is worn out. The truth is that given the proper set of circumstances, any living fossil can thrive and multiply.

Rescued from Extinction

THE METASEQUOIA

In 1941, a Japanese scientist, Shigeru Niki of Kyoto University, finished writing a paper about sequoias and sequoia-like trees that were older than the sequoias of California. In the paper he called one type of ancient sequoia a "metasequoia." It had lived 20 million years ago and was thought now to be extinct. After studying numerous fossils, Niki had concluded that the metasequoia was not a sequoia tree, although very closely related to one. He never dreamed that there were metasequoias living on earth. But there were.

Sequoias are gigantic trees; many get to be over 350 feet high. There are two types: the redwoods, which grow along the California seacoast, and another type, big trees with huge trunks which grow in the mountains of California. They have red wood and so are sometimes called redwoods. They are conifers and have small cones. Their leaves look a little bit like pine needles, but are smaller and flatter.

Niki did not know it, but in the rainy hills of China, at Wanshien and nearby, not far from the deep, rugged gorge of the Yangtze River, some tall trees were growing. The Chinese called them "shui-sa," which means water pine. Many Chinese revered the trees; there were shrines at the bases of some. These trees were metasequoias, and they were threatened.

China had been at war with Japan and was now involved in a civil war. Lumber was desperately needed. Near Wanshien, gangs of workers cut down metasequoias right and left. Those with shrines were spared; so were a few deep in forests.

In February, 1946, a Chinese forester, Wang-chan, was in the region of Wanshien. He examined the trees and suspected that they were unknown to scientists and had therefore never been given a scientific name. That was odd, because botanists from China and other countries had explored the area several times before, searching for unusual trees and plants. After Wang-chan announced that he had found an unusual tree, he sent twigs, cones, and leaves to several noted botanists. One of them was Dr. Hsen-hsu Hu of Peking. Dr. Hsen-hsu Hu was familiar with the paper which Niki had written, and he immediately realized that the twigs, cones, and leaves were from a metasequoia.

News of the trees spread quickly around the world. In early
1948, Ralph W. Chaney, an American professor, went to China
to study the metasequoias. He planned to take photographs of
them and collect their seeds. But China was deep in civil war
by then, so travel was hard and dangerous. Chaney went by
boat up rivers and by foot over slippery trails high above deep
canyons. He walked 125 miles through country that almost no
one but the Chinese natives had ever seen. By the time Chaney
saw his first metasequoia, Chinese botanists whom he had
met a few weeks earlier had told him that only about one thousand were left on earth.

Chaney saw that the best metasequoias were protected by
priests in temple yards. He was familiar with sequoias and
trees related to them, and he believed that some of the trees
were several centuries old. The tallest tree was 98 feet high.
This is not particularly high when we consider the redwoods
often tower over 300 feet. Nevertheless, it was a tall tree, as tall
as a large white oak. Chaney found out that unlike most conifers, often called evergreens, the metasequoia lost its needles
in wintertime.

Chaney brought seeds back to the United States and sent
others to various countries. In May, 1948, seeds were planted at
the U.S. Government Plant Introduction Garden in Glenn Dale,
Maryland. Others were planted in Kew Gardens, England. No
one knew whether or not the seeds would sprout. But, four

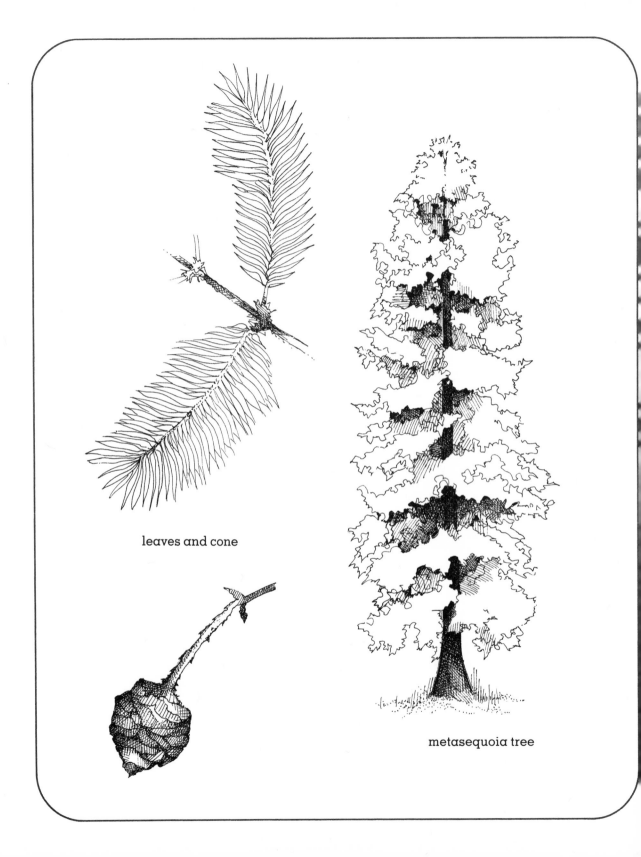

leaves and cone

metasequoia tree

months later, healthy seedlings were growing. Some were shipped to Alaska. Why Alaska? From fossil evidence, scientists knew that metasequoias had once grown in that region. They also knew that the weather in southern Alaska was similar to that in Wanshien. They guessed that Alaska would be an ideal place for them, and they were right. Today a large number of metasequoias are growing in Alaska, and in other places as well. Several grow in Brooklyn, New York, because the Brooklyn Botanic Gardens once gave away seedlings in a drive for donations.

The metasequoia had been rescued from extinction in the very nick of time. It is more than likely that eventually all would have been cut down, even those protected by shrines, because the side that won China's civil war did away with many such shrines and temples. All this might have happened if Dr. Hsen-hsu Hu had not identified the contents of the package from Wang-chan. Fortunately, the leaders of China today do protect the trees. The oldest of all still grow in and around Wanshien.

As botanists have had more time to study the metasequoia, they have realized that it is not quite as closely related to the sequoia as was once thought. It is probably more directly related to a type of cypress tree, the bald cypress, which grows in the southern swamps of America. The bald cypress has leaves that resemble pine needles, small cones, and huge roots that

rise up above the ground in knobs called "knees." Like the metasequoia, the bald cypress also loses its leaves in winter.
These leaves and cones look like those of the metasequoia, but
the metasequoias do not have knees on their roots, and their
trunks are straighter and their branches small and thinner.

We are lucky to have the metasequoia. It is a magnificent-
looking tree, which will grace many parks and lawns. Each
year, as more seeds are planted in various parts of the world,
they become more common.

Believed to Be Extinct

THE COELACANTH

No living fossil is as famous as the coelacanth (pronounced see-lah-kanth). Its discovery made headlines all over the world. Although the story of the coelacanth is well known, it is worth telling again, because it is one of the most exciting biology stories of all time.

Fish first appeared on earth between 405 and 345 million years ago, during the Devonian age. Because so many fish evolved then, the Devonian age is often called the Age of Fish. The fish at that time were different from most fish today. Some were armored. Others had scales, but the scales were very large. As a rule of thumb, one can say that fish with large scales go back further in time than most others.

Scientists who studied fossils from the Devonian period

were familiar with fossils of a fish called the coelacanth. It was a fish with large scales, a large, fleshy tail with a fringe of spines, and fins more like flippers than ordinary fish fins. Its head was large in relation to its body, and it possessed a set of lungs in addition to gills. The coelacanth was a member of a group of fish, called lobe-fin fish, believed to have been the link between fish and amphibians; the legs of amphibians are thought to have evolved from the stubby fins of the lobe-fin fish.

No scientist ever expected to see a coelacanth alive. It would have been less surprising to see a living dinosaur, since dinosaurs are more recent creatures in terms of geological time, having walked the earth 175 million years after the Devonian age ended. But unexpected things can happen.

On December 22, 1938, a small fishing boat was sailing in the Indian Ocean off the coast of South Africa. The fishermen were hauling up nets, which contained quite a number of fish. One of the fish was very unusual. It was four and a half feet long and had blue eyes and large bluish scales the color of steel. The fish snapped at anyone who got near it and managed to live for three hours out of the water. It was indeed a fierce, tough creature.

The captain of the vessel realized that he had caught a remarkable fish, and he thought that he might make some money from it if he took it to a museum. When the boat arrived in East

London, South Africa, he telephoned the East London Museum and told a Miss M. Courtenay-Latimer about the fish. As a matter of routine, she asked that it be brought to the museum.

It was not uncommon for curators at the museum, including Miss Latimer, to receive reports of strange fish. But this time she could have no idea how important the fish would be.

When the captain arrived with the fish, Miss Latimer knew immediately that she had never seen anything else like it alive. She had seen drawings of fish from the Devonian age, and she guessed that the fish might be prehistoric. And, although she did not consider herself an expert on prehistoric fish, her hunch proved correct.

Unfortunately, it was a hot day and the fish was decaying at a rapid rate. Its stink was awful. Miss Latimer realized that she had to act swiftly to save as much as she could, so she grabbed a pencil and paper and quickly sketched it. After the drawing was done, she had the fish's guts cut out and thrown away. The skin and skull were preserved. Then she dashed off a letter to Dr. J. L. B. Smith in Grahamstown, South Africa. Dr. Smith, the country's leading expert on fish, was there for Christmas vacation. The mail was so slow that the letter containing the sketch of the fish remained unopened for a long time.

When Dr. Smith finally received the letter and drawing, he realized that the fish was a coelacanth. But they had died out 130 million years ago, during the Cretaceous period, or so sci-

coelacanth

entists believed. His head spun. Dr. Smith later reported that he had said to himself, "Such things cannot be."

As quickly as he could, Dr. Smith traveled to East London. There Miss Latimer showed him the skull and skin of the fish. They were enough for a positive identification. He gave the fish its scientific name, *Latimeria chalumnae,* in honor of Miss Latimer. *Chalumnae* refers to the Chalumna River, near where the fish was caught. Within hours, newspaper headlines all over the world proclaimed the astonishing news.

Dr. Smith examined the remains of the fish as thoroughly as he could. He talked to the fishermen about the fish's behavior while it had been alive and got as much information as possible. But mostly he wanted to see one alive himself. He questioned dozens of fishermen about the possibility of catching another. From the answers he received, Dr. Smith realized that such a fish was rare, but as he stood on the shore and looked out over the ocean he knew that there obviously had to be others.

Along with several museums, Dr. Smith offered a reward of $400, a lot of money in those days, to anyone who caught a coelacanth. He had thousands of leaflets printed up in English, Portuguese, and French. They were posted in cafes, fish markets, on boats, and handed to fishermen on docks up and down the coast. In spite of the reward and leaflets, fourteen years passed before the next coelacanth was caught.

In 1952, a fisherman from the Comores Islands caught another coelacanth. Dr. Smith's leaflets had instructed fishermen to pack the fish in ice, but since this fisherman had no ice, he packed it in salt and injected it with formaldehyde. Dr. Smith had all sorts of difficulties arranging a trip to the Comores, which are about two thousand miles from Grahamstown, but eventually he got there.

The fish was in a boat and wrapped in a newspaper. Dr. Smith was so excited and nervous that he could not unwrap the fish. It had to be done for him. Once it was unwrapped, Dr. Smith looked down on an animal that was thought to have disappeared from earth 130 million years ago. He was so overcome that he knelt down and wept.

What made it possible for generations and generations of coelacanth to survive down through the ages? Its local environment in the Indian Ocean may have remained relatively unchanged since the Devonian age, including temperature, salinity, mineral content, oxygen, and so forth. Either that, or the fish was able to migrate to areas where the water was suitable. And, obviously, it has been able to successfully compete for its share of the food supply. For these and perhaps for other unknown reasons, the coelacanth has survived on earth for over 400 million years.

Index

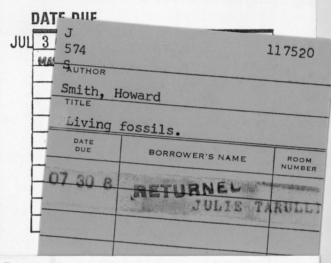